Mario Petrucci

FEARNOUGHT

POEMS FOR SOUTHWELL WORKHOUSE

THE
NATIONAL
TRUST

FEARNOUGHT

POEMS FOR SOUTHWELL WORKHOUSE

First published in 2006 through the National Trust

© Mario Petrucci 2006

ISBN: (10 digit) 1-84359-251-7 (13 digit) 978-1-84359-251-8

http://mariopetrucci.port5.com

By the same author:

Shrapnel and Sheets. Headland, 1996. Poetry Book Society Recommendation.

Bosco. Hearing Eye, 1999 & 2001. Book-length sequence on deforestation.

Lepidoptera. KT Publications, 1999 & 2001; Kite Modern Poetry Series 88 & 96 (limited editions). Experimental prose and science-based poetry.

The Stamina of Sheep, published in conjunction with **The Havering Poetry Study Pack**. The London Borough of Havering 2002 (limited edition).

Heavy Water: a poem for Chernobyl. Enitharmon Press, 2004. Winner of the 2002 Daily Telegraph/ Arvon Prize.

Half Life. Heaventree Press, 2004. Sister publication to *Heavy Water*.

Catullus. Perdika Press, 2006. Adaptations with original Latin facing.

Also: **Heavy Water: a film for Chernobyl**. Seventh Art Productions, 2006.

Designed, and typeset in Times New Roman, by Mario Petrucci.
Printed in Great Britain by Catford Print Centre.

Acknowledgements

Some kind of special award needs to be invented for, and bestowed upon, Sarah Clarke, Nikki Williams and colleagues at Southwell Workhouse for their faith in this project, and for so impressively slip-catching all my off-line-and-length queries. I am grateful, too, to John and Jill Pepper who gave helpful (and often colourful) advice on local diction. My thanks to the National Trust for hosting the residency and to Nottinghamshire County Council for its support (administered through Ross Bradshaw and the utterly indispensable Chris Jones). My deep appreciation, finally, to Martyn Crucefix, Philip Gross, Chris Jones, Francesca Stregapede and Brett Van Toen for many valuable comments – and to Anne and Peter for enduring, so patiently, such frequent ritual transmogrification into poetic sounding boards.

Photography: Kate Fisher and Mario Petrucci.

CONTENTS

Foreword: the Southwell Workhouse
Poetry Residency 2004 / 2005

Early in this residency, I was struck by the potential of Southwell Workhouse as a 'text gallery'. Its expanses of brickwork painted just short of anaemia – all those uncluttered ceilings and floors – presented themselves receptively for the hanging of poems. I say *receptively* rather than passively because, paradoxical as it may seem, those apparently neutral surfaces can act as sounding boards, as 'amplifiers', for stray thoughts and musings. That quality is rare in a museum: the capacity not only to speak, but to listen. We all know the best listeners make us talk. In fact, the structure was (for me) such an ardent listener I had to maintain a careful distance. Even the briefest of visits could yield a stone-swell of ideas, as though those flagstones were really the grey, deceptive surface of an easily defrosted sea. More than once, I felt that sharp flutter peculiar to swimmers who, on the brink of being overwhelmed, had previously thought of themselves as experienced.

I have tried to reveal – and exploit – all of that. Indeed, the nature, content and mood of these poems express how the rooms and yards insisted upon (or generated) a sort of 'negative capability' within me: not quite in the way Keats meant the term, but in my having to let these two fat leaves of brain open up to receive what darkness or light the house had on offer, without needing (at least, not initially) the usual swarm of facts, dates, incidents. This is somewhat knuckle-to-brow, I know – a quintessentially Romantic position; though also a potent one. It responds to the invitation to approach such spaces not fact-first but sense-first, heart-first. Information is essential, of course; and yet, it provides only part of the learning experience. We must also take on board that the initial 'sense impact' of a space is what sometimes motivates us to find out more about it.

With a conservation period intersecting Dickens' heyday, and given its reputation as the best specimen of its kind in the country, Southwell Workhouse might have seemed ripe for a stuffing of juicy artefacts or crowd-pleasing tableaux and recreations. It is audacious – almost outrageous – to present the visitor, instead, with so very little. It works. The few objects one does find, accrue a strange intensity. There were occasions, no doubt, when the kitchen or yards would have heaved with workhouse activity; but the decision to allow the building, now, simply to stand *per se* delivers to even the casual visitor a charge that is more artistic than curatorial. It cuts closer to the psychological truth of living in segregation. It also removes us from the notion of a museum as period entertainment supplied through a series of semi-educational set pieces, leading us instead towards education as an immersion in history via internalised imaginative encounters. It helped save me from slipping into facile, or over-fastidious, poetic reconstructions of the mid-nineteenth century. It saved the site from becoming an old curiosity shop of artefacts or (to reprise that sometimes unsavoury word I used earlier) a 'specimen' of glass cases and desiccated captions. I very much wanted to respond to the house in these – its own – terms; and so I let *Fearnought* be moulded by that absence of occupants with their life-baggage of furniture, papers and other paraphernalia.

There is one absence in this book, however, that demands I say more about my decision against 'facile, or over-fastidious, poetic reconstructions'. It is the absence of dialect. This part of the country abounds with its own words and pronunciations (as highlighted, for instance, by John Beeton) and I was hoping to draw on the fascinating word-hoard of 'Nottinghamese'. Sadly, I found it difficult to acquire any sense of the Southwell dialect as it was around 1840, and it would have been entirely cod to drop in the odd researched phrase here and there just to confer regional or historical flavour. That is not how locals would have spoken and, in any case,

I probably would have misused those phrases, or trampled their subtleties, through ignorance. In short, I simply was not qualified to use dialect in an authentic, thoroughgoing way. Moreover, tripping up readers (especially younger ones) with arcane words and thickets of footnotes would have overturned any benefits. Some *Fearnought* poems do speak 'in voice'; but here (excepting the vagrant Martha who has travelled, audibly, from the east of London) I stretch the tongue in mild ways that merely suggest a general sense of 'otherness', of people in another age. Clearly, these characters aim to inhabit the time period of the house (a house, by the way, not without its own temporal idiosyncrasies); but I did not want their voices, or this book as a whole, to be chained there. Sarah, for example, would have had to wait until about 1918 for the word *posh* as we now understand it (though it did have earlier incarnations as 'a dandy' or as thieves' slang for money). As I say, fastidious realism was not my chief aim. Naturally, I did what I could to avoid blatant offences against etymology or factual accuracy; but I also desired a language working at its contemporary best.

Moving on to other species of absence, there is certainly an odd richness behind the spareness you encounter at Southwell Workhouse, not dissimilar to the (often misunderstood) vacancies of meditation or those freewheeling moods set in train by certain types of chant. The space can even engender something akin to *echolalia* (but productively so, rather than dysfunctionally) in the way it seems to lower your threshold of awareness for recurrent subliminal impressions and feelings. In spite of this – or perhaps because of it – the workhouse was not an altogether easy poetic residence. With mantras and meditation you can lead yourself to exasperation and boredom as well as to heightened responsiveness; likewise, this house. Those wonderfully amplifying walls can also shut you into a brittle, deadening silence. Against all the fecundity I have pointed to, I must admit such emptiness can sometimes feel debilitating, overly absorptive, or too fugitive or arbitrary in what it suggests. The dual challenge, then – as was apparent, too, some years ago in my Imperial War Museum residency – was to remain germane and focused whilst generating the kind of gentle excitement that draws flitting eyes and ears nearer in: close or intent enough, in fact, to… *dwell.* The contexts of these two museums, however, could not be more dissimilar: glutted with historical booty, the war museum offers a hornets' nest of ideas and visual stories; the workhouse is more like a shoebox full of hibernating snails. That last image carries no hint of criticism on its back, I promise. If, at first sight, the workhouse appears a rigid or uneventful place, just disturb the box, unfreeze it a little in the imagination, and its slow muscular outpouring becomes inexorable: "drenched there with purpose... a snail's fury", to adopt some lines from the poet Thom Gunn.

I did realise of course, quite rapidly, that the poems would need a hefty dose of realism, with human stories of genuine particularity and engagement. I hope I have demonstrated, though, how it also dawned on me, quietly, that there was ample room here for a divergent strain of reality, conveyed in fragments of language more elusive and, somehow, ajar. Apart from stimulating contemplation, questioning, curiosity and multiple readings, this latter type of poem might offer an altogether different set of 'ways in' to the workhouse and its various associations. I have come to think of these poems as *porticelle:* 'little doors'. I am sure visitors will be, as I was, both moved and appalled at the many stories the workhouse yields, if only we meet it half-way and give an ounce of effort; but it is the *porticelle* within *Fearnought* – those open-ended, semi-narrative or non-narrative poems – that reflect (each with its distinctive hue) an equally profound quality of this space: a place whose poverty filled my imaginative pockets, whose boundedness proliferated forms. In being exposed to the superficial nullity of Southwell Workhouse, by walking through its many room- and corridor-sized echo chambers, I have been greatly privileged and enriched.

Mario Petrucci

Poet in Residence
Southwell Workhouse

Autumn 2005

"An empty workhouse is a successful workhouse."

The Reverend J.T. Becher
Founder of Southwell Workhouse

RISING BELL

ROLL OVER !

There were ten in the bed
and the little one said –

Roll over! Roll over!
So they all rolled over

and he fell out.

*Huddersfield township workhouse slept as many as 10 children per
bed. Southwell Workhouse, too, suffered periods of overcrowding.*

FEARNOUGHT

Mornings
when I pull on this
jacket

I feel
through scuppered heels
each flagstone

melt. Melt
and rock to the greys
of sea. See how

they clad
me as they do the rest –
as they would

a winter vessel –
in wool wove stiff as
sheet metal against

cold so
fierce as to make flesh
turn against itself.

Yet even
the Queen's ship must
wait its tide

and I
await mine. With their
jacket I berth my

self against labour –
in this fleet ebb of life
resist each

rough swell.

*Fearnought (or Fernought) was a coarse woollen
insulation for ships in the Arctic, sometimes used
to make hard-wearing jackets for workhouse men.*

BW + B

One
black skirt.
Two

white
pinafores. Two
blue

blouses –
gingham. Black
stockings.

White
cotton caps. A pair.
Blue

woollen
shawl.   There –
see it

true. How
each day they
make me

Black
White and
Blue.

LEAD

Lead on the rooftop
Lead in the grate

Lead on the tongue-tip
Lead on your plate

Lead in your pillowcase
Lead in your head –

All of us listless
And all of us lead

MORNING

and east brims with
honey – the windows
with curd

all night the stars
spooned sweet crystals
through grass

a sun yolkless with
winter breaks in
its saucer

and those cellar stones
settle under froths
of cocoa

But such thoughts are
flies – drawn all
plying yet

drowsy to glass (those
tiny blows – each
hollow butt)

till half-cured they
fall punch-drunk
through

that light

FOOD

AND

PRAYER

Even this Earth
must yield a little
at every step we take.
Can't you feel? –

or hear our dead:
their tiny time-
shrunk moans
filtering up

through clay, loam
made dense with flesh
and bone – just
to support us?

BREAD

We're men half-
baked – swinging
lead-heavy sledges

over our heads
on elbowy sticks
of bread. Hour

by hour: men
of flour. Saved by
a pinch of salt.

Here because
we ought to use
our loaf. Because

men of fire eat
iron. Rust. Entire
nations. But we

float through days
on crusts. Dawn
to dusk each raft

the same. Like
us. Each slice we
are – adrift on

a basin of gruel.
Breakfast. Dinner.
Supper. One fuel.

And when at last
we rise to heaven
then I suppose

we'll be made
to mow His fields
divine with wheat –

move mountains
of holy yeast – and
reach back down

to knead (one
by one) each grey
cloud of dough.

The staple of the workhouse diet was bread.
'Sledge' = sledgehammer.

GRUEL CAULDRON

To make one gallon
you must sink a pound
of oatmeal. Pour a half

ladle of treacle. Add
anything up to a palmful
of salt. Though here they

take much greater pains:
mete these out to the grain
precise as punishment.

All into their cauldron.
Only flame will lick it
with relish. Soot rind

on the outside – grey
phlegm within: just as we
become in the breaking

of years stone by stone.
Whoever praises gruel has
lost a tongue. One may

walk to the cauldron with
a gentleman's bearing –
but away from there

a pauper runs. As often
as you drink (or swill till
belly swells to the pot's

pink reflection – taut as
pigskin stretched on iron)
still you draw there

no satisfaction. They have
forged a bottomless mouth.
The deepest well of nill.

Nill: a disinclination or aversion to something (1677).

SHANTY

Make me a mast
from a long man's bones

Make me a deck
from weeks of work

Make me a helm
from the rubbed-off

skins of oakum
Carve me a rudder

from doors that sever
sister from brother

Make me an anchor

Stitch me a sail
from peelings of spud

shaved so thin
they show the light –

a sail that light it
billows on a sneeze

But don't do
these – just break

that window
Give me

a breeze

SUB ROSA

That grille in the ceiling
is a black
rose —

flower of my name under
distemper
– yet

past those chill petals (more
a daisy's now I
look)

hopes rise quick as warmth
– though so many
words

here have risen and been lost
I have no throat to
speak

with my husband the other side
of walls and heart a
bud

black with the worry that now he
loves me – he loves me
not

Sub rosa (Latin) means 'under the rose', an emblem of secrecy.
Distemper: a water-based paint, as well as a deranged state.

SARAH

*"The use of knives and forks was unknown to them ...
It required practice to enable them to get up and down stairs."*

On ex-workhouse girls in domestic service.

Crock-breaker they call me.
Butter fingers. *Useless for service*
says Mistress. Always falling. Never

seen no forks nor knifes before
that morning. Nor silver. Had to
touch to check they was real. Reckon

I been falling all me life. That
work house first – this posh house
now – seems every house must have

its Master. Not my fault I'm
pretty. This head of curls. Fat
fist of good they done me. Falling

Sarah. And Master – when we
pass at the corner – wall to wall. Worse
than a boulder. *Butter fingers* says Mistress

scoffing butter. She don't know
the end of it. This pinny beginning to
hug me belly. In this house – the grime

behind each brick. No point
ruing it. Nothing else doing. I have
to keep falling. To be rid of it. Falling

down Master's stairs.

STAIRS

STAIRS I

Here
we are the law.
Not just of where

to walk
but how to
look. So stare at

us well
because we lack
soft landings. Keep

eyes to
the floor or we'll
trip you back down –

plus a
bloody nose.
Let the earliest riser

among you
sneak up on us.
You'll find us always

on guard.
We will never
budge. Every step

you take
will make you
toe our same old line.

Each little
flight you fancy
returns you a grudge.

STAIRS II

Each little flight you
fancy returns you
a grudge.

Every step you take
will make you toe
our same old

line. You'll find us
always on guard.
We will never

budge. Let the earliest
riser among you
sneak up on

us: we'll trip you back
down. Or a bloody
nose – *plus*. So

keep eyes to the floor.
Stare at us well
because

we lack soft landings.
Not just of where
to walk but

how to look. We
are here. The
Law.

STAIRS III

Every flight you fancy
will turn you. Each
little grudge –

a step you take. We'll
find you: make you
same. Older.

On guard. Toes always
in line. Our will
never budges.

Let us rise among you
alert – so *other*. But
sneak up (all

he-nose) – we'll trip
you back down to
blood-stark eyes.

Just keep to landings.
Look at us. *Stop.*
Here floors of

wet can walk before
you. How so?
Well – we

tut. Cause. We
are law. The
Here.

HOUSE

BRICKS AND CORTEX

This house is
brainy – given the right
half is wo

-men it
follows the left has to be
men (yes it

depends wh-
ich way you look:) but still
we've a devil's

body of brick
with wings tacked on from t-
woo quite different

birds – and stairs
whose nervy grey cascades of
ends pulse their

dark electrics
through each absence which
means a heart

or take us down
with cellars whose smelling
walls and wells

suggest the skull
that generates this telling
division of storeys

MULTIPLE CHOICE

My ceilings are high.
Why?

(a) It was the style.
(b) So rooms don't smell.
(c) For sense of space.
(d) To draw down Grace.
(e) So I'll impress.
(f) More is less.
(g) To feign a church.
(h) To swing the birch.
(i) Say *Ahh.* Don't know.

HAIKU

Each ribbed ceiling –
an iron lung
leached of breath.

PLAN

Believe me – I'm
  ordered. No play in

this lay-out: cross-
    section like cells

in a power plant.
    A line reflects me

left to right. I'm
    a Rorschach test

without a trace of
    butterfly – all but

mathematical.
    Each wall counts.

Look again. Zoom
    out – to how I

pattern the land.
      Shh. I have

a plan. One dusk
    I'll yank myself

up by my own dust
  and stone – trailing

coppery roots of
    cable and pipe as I

lift into that dark or-
    biting earth. Once

more I'll survey:
    be the light you

might mistake for
    a travelling star

as I move in
    the night the way

a planet does – until
    you sense I run

against. Have gone
    too fast. Too far.

Rorschach test: a standard set of symmetrical ink-blots, presented
for interpretation to someone undergoing psychoanalysis.

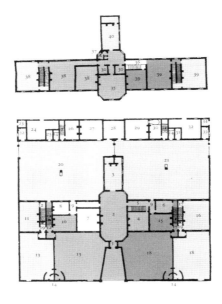

PAINTWORK

Look at me – slapped
on these walls. Take one
flake to examine in microscopes

sideways on. Read me. As if I
were the stuck-together pages
of a primer. Between my

layers of distemper find
litter of skin. A hair's blond
tail curled round its mousy follicle.

Let your laboratory eyes feast
on sweat pressed to the odd
gobbet of tar beneath

my sediments. Note
each thin black seam of
boredom. Year by year I grew

strange as a tree whose nested watch-
springs learned to unwind and
lay themselves flush.

Now I sleep an ugly skin-
deep sleep. You try to bring
me round – to guess four-square

lives from my jigsawed film. No
need. Just get close and sniff.
Take me in like home-

-eopathy. I'll crack
you up. Heal you. Give you
a fresh coat – one molecule at a time.

*To keep the men occupied, workhouse walls were given an annual
coat of 'distemper' (a cheap water-based paint). Tiny particles
from their environment are trapped between the layers.*

Am I a wall
– just a wall

in a Workhouse?
When it comes to

labour I might
offer some

shoulder to
cry on

I

can even
hold things up

when you have to
get round me – but

if you're looking
for blame   Don't

pin it
on

me

WORK

AND

REST

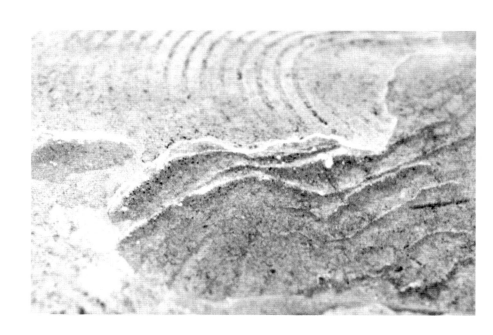

FLAGSTONE /
AMMONITE

Split this house as
if a stone – strike it

with attention's edge
so where it cleaves (a-

long this slab / be-
hind that wall) is all

you get of creatured
bodies soft as yours

but caught between
twin rocks in times

more hard – whose
dreams were claws

of hammer-chisel
moving slow with

muddied light and
trailing grooves that

even scabs of time
can't heal.   We at

least may choose: to
step right over or else

to use our hands these
vital hands as trowels

and every eye a living
pick uncovering how

each blow of work has
left its arc. Stoop low

enough. *Here.* And you
may see (who knows)

how life went cold.

SWEEPING

To get to know a house
you must sweep it. Make

stone darken with the broom.
It changes you – all that

dust. Call me loon if you
like – but I reckon there's

people in it. I've seen them
rise. Men on all fours the size

of carthorses. Backs steaming.
Women with limbs like jennies

who spin for the Devil. That
Master gets us all in the end.

Me? I've wept enough to damp
down this tuppence of dirt when

my turn comes. But if I can wear
every broom to its stub – maybe

these flags will become a grey
paper – be kind to a pauper

and give.

GRAFFITO

```
W O R C
  W O R D
    W O R D
      S O R D
      S W O R D
```

```
        W
        O
LEISURE E
        K
```

VAGRANT

Martha. That's the name
they puts down. Ain't never known
me real name – I mean the one me mother

must 'ave gave me. In London Town
me four walls was alleys. Me
ceilings was weather.

It weren't like I didn't 'ave
no friends – but if some gentleman
'appened to pass an' tossed us a penny

we was after it all cats-n-nails – friends
or no friends. So I gets to travelling
an' I ends up 'ere. *Martha*

they writes when I says I ain't
got no name. Same as Scripture –
that black book of theirs – gold edges –

pages like ants been crossing 'em with
muddy clogs.   Tomorrow they
chucks me out – but tonight

I'm warm a bit an' I gets to
eat off me own plate an' some right
royal girlie does me 'air with a proper brush.

Funny though – to 'ave just the one
name. *Martha*. When I says it it
rattles in me mouth like I'm

talking about some dead sister
– or like it was kept for 'undreds of
years in the gob of old Mother 'Ubbard.

Days like this when nothing much 'appens
an' it 'appens all day I remembers
being out on the Town doing

pockets or lifting – an' the way
them shopkeepers'd come running
in their aprons. Running after to call me

everything under God's sun.

*Vagrants: travellers who would arrive from all over the country.
They were segregated and allowed to stay only one night, perhaps
two, at a time.*

STONE-BREAKER

This ain't no show of force.
Men more muscled than I-is

gets trapped in their blows.
See? It's all in the weight an'

sweep of the sledge. How
you lets the silvery head find

her own sweet way to that
crack. When she goes like

that – so neat you feels it
in your blood – it's akin to

joy to watch them melons
split. 'Cause you knows

even stone more dirty an'
cheap than you-is can rock

isself to sleep in its halves
clean as two moons – two

moons made of lime.

NIGHTFALL

FIRST SNOW

Winter bedtime in Southwell Workhouse was 8pm to 7am.

*It was not unknown in workhouse infirmaries
for a living patient to share a bed with a dead body.*

I wait. Half the two faces of

that clock. Half my God-given
right spent abed – half this life

willing each ember in my grate
not to die down. Bedded here

with legs and arms of lard till
done for – half-froze with this

corpse beside me who was once
Old Jack – who cooled so long

before twelve it seemed another
night entire to that first stroke.

Tonight. Perhaps it will fall
tonight. That feathered world –

its air of mint.   I lie in sheets
grey as slush. Half awake. Half

lead. Half dreaming me outside
with this body cold as starch

in its crisp bed.

BADGERS

You made us out so black
and white. It must have
seemed quite slight

to some. A square of
copper stamped at the neck.
A red and blue weal raised on

one shoulder. That yellow dapple –
not of angled sun – but your
jaundice of *Juden*. So

many markings. You
wedged us in brown. Green.
Purple. The pink inverted triangle –

the black inverted triangle. Follow
these far enough back and
in – and who would

dare split *us* from
you? Still our outside-
in coats drew those searchlight

eyes – dark beams sweeping
corridor and kerb till we
became the beast you

first saw. Poor Badgers
that you are – forever passing on
old wounds. Night upon

night – each mind purblind to
difference stitching there
its latest shade so that

when again you take aim
you'll see no blood – will see
us plain – in that narrowed sight.

*Under the 1697 Act, those receiving parish relief had to have a red
or blue badge on their right shoulder.*

*Slave badges, made of copper alloy, were common in Charleston
(South Carolina).*

*In Nazi Germany, Jews ('Juden') were forced to wear a yellow star.
In the concentration camps, prisoners were identified as homosexual,
Romany, antisocial, etc. via triangular badges of various colours.*

NIGHT TRAIN

Neville Chamberlain's 'The Local Government Act' (1929) aimed for widespread reform of the workhouse system. It took many years to bite.

Some bloke must've
put me on rails – chuffed with my
low train of thought

You stoke me

This Way to make'em
grovel – to steam those same few
lines into the poor

You shovel it

Now your guv'nor says
whoa! – thinks he can brake me
with new law

You make me

But I'll mow I'll
whistle through sleepers – miles
of rot before

You'll blow it

I stop

DAGUERREOTYPE

An early form of photograph on silver-plated copper.

It must have been taken
when photography
was a youngster

– the camera awkward
as a foal on un-
equal legs –

but still its oblong of silver
brings you to this
row of faces

now dun with age &
caught in a snap
so cold so

real you swear your own
wrists chafe from
their cuffs

of coarse cotton. That's
what makes you
peer again –

slant it to the window
for whiter light as
you feel

the draught from thin
glass down that
shoulder

then notice how below
in the courtyard
nobody

moves.   Squint closer.
For that one face
(extreme left)

halved by the edge –
a face that can
only be

yours. Be
yours. Forget
the exposure as you

grapple
to remember. Why
can't you remember your

name? And
God – shouldn't there
be someone else in this room?

In this house?

NIGHTLIGHT

In eyes half shut
it's a distant sun
or a close-up star.

Nurse shuffles her
rounds – grey moth
dusted with dusk

too tired to fly.
Shadows dissolve.
She strikes a lucifer

to the very lamp
that will draw
and keep her.

Her light opens –
fragrant on the eye.
Against the dark

one night flower.

'Lucifer' – a primitive match, ignited by friction.